ROCKETS

David Baker and
Heather Kissock

MEDIA ENHANCED BOOKS
AV²
BY WEIGL
ADDED VALUE · AUDIO VISUAL

www.av2books.com

AV² provides enriched content that supplements and complements this book. Weigl's AV² books strive to create inspired learning and engage young minds in a total learning experience.

Your AV² Media Enhanced books come alive with...

Audio
Listen to sections of the book read aloud.

Key Words
Study vocabulary, and complete a matching word activity.

Video
Watch informative video clips.

Quizzes
Test your knowledge.

Go to www.av2books.com, and enter this book's unique code.

BOOK CODE

G787774

Embedded Weblinks
Gain additional information for research.

Slide Show
View images and captions, and prepare a presentation.

AV² by Weigl brings you media enhanced books that support active learning.

Try This!
Complete activities and hands-on experiments.

... and much, much more!

Published by AV² by Weigl
350 5th Avenue, 59th Floor
New York, NY 10118
Website: www.av2books.com

Library of Congress Cataloging-in-Publication Data

Names: Baker, David, 1944- author. | Kissock, Heather, author.
Title: Rockets / David Baker, Heather Kissock.
Description: New York, NY : AV2 by Weigl, 2017. | Series: All about space science | Includes index.
Identifiers: LCCN 2016054639 (print) | LCCN 2017002157 (ebook) | ISBN 9781489658210 (hard cover : alk. paper) | ISBN 9781489658227 (soft cover : alk. paper) | ISBN 9781489658234 (Multi-user ebk.)
Subjects: LCSH: Rockets (Aeronautics)--Juvenile literature. | Outer space--Exploration--Juvenile literature.
Classification: LCC TL782.5 .B35 2017 (print) | LCC TL782.5 (ebook) | DDC 629.47/5--dc23
LC record available at https://lccn.loc.gov/2016054639

Printed in the United States of America in Brainerd, Minnesota
1 2 3 4 5 6 7 8 9 0 21 20 19 18 17

032017
020117

Editor: Katie Gillespie
Art Director: Terry Paulhus

Photo Credits
Every reasonable effort has been made to trace ownership and to obtain permission to reprint copyright material. The publishers would be pleased to have any errors or omissions brought to their attention so that they may be corrected in subsequent printings.

Weigl acknowledges Getty Images, iStock, Alamy, Newscom, and Shutterstock as its primary image suppliers for this title.

ALL ABOUT SPACE SCIENCE

ROCKETS

CONTENTS

What Is a Rocket?

Arocket is a powerful means of launching things over great distances. There are many types of rocket. A firework for parties and celebrations is a type of rocket. It is small and flies within the **atmosphere**. Other types of rocket include those that are designed to work in space.

The first space shuttle was launched on April 12, 1981. Astronauts Robert Crippen and John Young orbited Earth for 54 hours.

Most rockets are tube-shaped devices that carry a special type of fuel, as well as oxygen to burn the fuel. Together, fuel and oxygen are called the **propellants**. They create the **thrust** to propel the rocket. When the fuel is ignited, gases are released. The force of these gases pushing in one direction causes the tube to move through the air in the opposite direction.

A rocket is the only device that can travel into space. This is because it is does not need air and does not rely on an external force for its power. Everything it needs to power itself is contained within the rocket.

The H1 liquid propellant rocket engine used kerosene and liquid oxygen.

MOVING OBJECTS

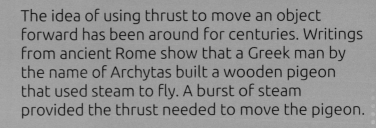

The idea of using thrust to move an object forward has been around for centuries. Writings from ancient Rome show that a Greek man by the name of Archytas built a wooden pigeon that used steam to fly. A burst of steam provided the thrust needed to move the pigeon.

About 300 years after Archytas built his pigeon, Hero of Alexandria invented a rocket-like device called an aeolipile. It also used steam to move objects.

Solid and Liquid Fueled Rockets

Rocket propellant can be solid or liquid. Solid propellant can take many forms. Some contain tiny grains of a powder that, when ignited, will burn fast with a bright flame. Fireworks are an example of this type of rocket. Another form of solid propellant is like a **resin**. Both types contain a combination of fuel and oxygen. Oxygen and fuel packed together make an **oxidizer**.

Some big solid propellant rockets are built from a series of hollow **cylindrical** sections, one placed on top of the other. There is a rubbery fuel inside the hollow of each cylinder. When ignited, the cylinders burn from the inside out, toward the wall of the cylinder. This produces thrust that escapes out the bottom. The National Aeronautics and Space Administration (NASA) used this kind of solid propellant rocket to launch shuttles into space.

Expedition 46 launched in December 2015. Crew members conducted human research, education activities, and physical science investigations.

In a liquid-propellant rocket, fuel is carried in one tank, and a substance that helps the fuel burn, such as oxygen, is carried in another. Both combine inside the engine to produce exhaust that acts as a propellant.

In 1232 BC, the **Chinese used rocket-arrows** propelled by burning gunpowder in their **war with the Mongols**.

Liquid-propellant rockets are most efficient and are best for space launches. This is because they produce more energy for the same weight of propellant than solid propellant rockets. This helps push them far into space without exhausting the fuel supply. Solid propellant rockets are best for use as **missiles** because they fire faster than liquid-propellant rockets and can gain speed more quickly during liftoff. In times of war, they can get to their target quickly.

The Saturn V rocket carries 318,000 gallons of liquid oxygen in its first stage. (1.2 million liters)

The most powerful rockets are called heavy lift launch vehicles.

Rocket Parts

Rockets come in a range of sizes and have many uses. Rockets that are sent into space, however, have four main parts. These parts are called systems. Each system has its own role in the operation of the rocket.

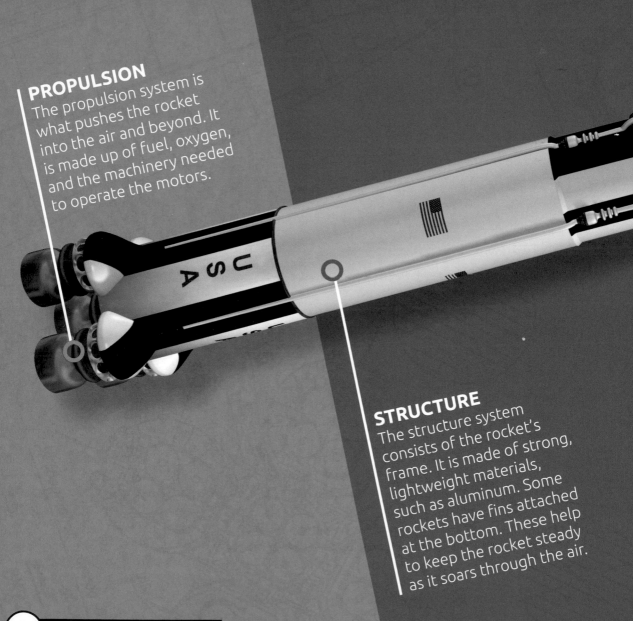

PROPULSION
The propulsion system is what pushes the rocket into the air and beyond. It is made up of fuel, oxygen, and the machinery needed to operate the motors.

STRUCTURE
The structure system consists of the rocket's frame. It is made of strong, lightweight materials, such as aluminum. Some rockets have fins attached at the bottom. These help to keep the rocket steady as it soars through the air.

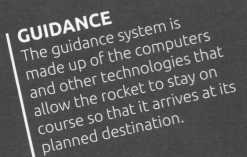

GUIDANCE
The guidance system is made up of the computers and other technologies that allow the rocket to stay on course so that it arrives at its planned destination.

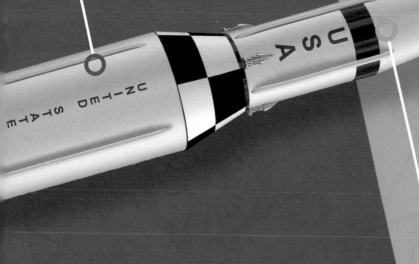

PAYLOAD
The payload system consists of the cargo the rocket is carrying into space. This can include **satellites** and humans.

BASICS OF THRUST

In 1686, Sir Isaac Newton, a British scientist, introduced his laws of motion. One of these laws explained how every action has an equal and opposite reaction. Rockets are an example of this law. A rocket engine produces the action of exhaust gases flowing out the back of the engine. In reaction, a thrusting force is produced in the opposite direction. This propels the rocket into space.

Action

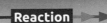

Reaction

Launching Satellites

In the 1950s, small rockets were being sent into space for research purposes. Some were launched with cameras that could look back at Earth. Others carried scientific tools that took measurements and recorded data related to Earth's atmosphere before falling back to Earth. These rockets were called "sounding rockets" because they helped scientists "sound out," or explore, the upper edges of Earth's atmosphere, also known as near-Earth space.

Development and use of sounding rockets gave scientists an interest in putting satellites in orbit. This would give the tools the rockets carried a permanent **platform** in space. The first country to achieve this goal was Russia, when, on October 4, 1957, it launched the first successful satellite, *Sputnik I*. A few months later, the United States sent their first satellite, *Explorer I*, into space.

Rockets are still used to launch satellites and other equipment into space. These rockets are often called launch vehicles. Since the first Russian satellite launched in 1957, countries around the world have been using launch vehicles to send satellites into space.

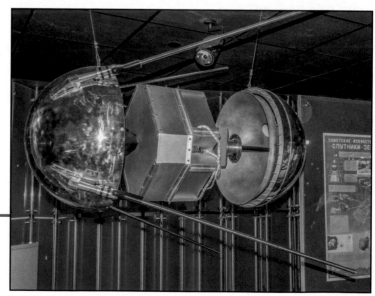

A replica of *Sputnik I* is on display at the Cosmonautics Memorial Museum in Moscow, Russia.

The rocket engines used for launching satellites are very powerful. The rocket acts as a motor to push the satellite upward. The entire structure of the rocket, including the motor and the fuel tanks, is called an **Expendable** Launch Vehicle, or ELV. The main body of the rocket separates from the satellite after it reaches orbit. When the launch vehicle and satellite reach orbit, the motor shuts down, and the satellite is released into space.

The Soyuz TMA-13 spacecraft launched from the Baikonur Cosmodrome in Kazakhstan on October 12, 2008.

Rockets from Russia

Like many other countries, Russia developed solid and liquid propellant rockets during World War II. After the war, Russia kept making rockets and missiles that could be used in the event of another war. One of the most important rockets to be made after the war was the R-7 intercontinental **ballistic missile** (ICBM). At first, it was designed to carry warheads as far as 5,468 miles (8,800 kilometers). However, the R-7 became better known as a satellite launcher. In fact, Russia used the R-7 to launch *Sputnik I* and other satellites into space. Over time, changes have been made to the rocket so that it has greater lifting power. Now called Soyuz, the rocket is still used to launch satellites and send astronauts from around the world to the International Space Station (ISS), a research center located in space.

Ten Proton missions were completed in 2013, including the delivery of the Astra 2E satellite.

Russia has built other rockets as well. The biggest Russian rocket is called Proton. It was designed in the early 1960s as a missile but was never used as one. Instead, it was made into an ELV for satellites and spacecraft. Proton made its first flight in 1965. With a thrust of 1,050 tons (953 tonnes), today's Proton-M models can put satellites weighing more than 20 tons (18.5 t) in orbit.

A still bigger rocket, called N1, also was built in the 1960s. It was meant to send Russian astronauts to the Moon. Only a few were built and tested, but they all failed shortly after launch. Production of the N1 stopped. Later, the ideas behind the N1 were used to make a rocket called Energia. Energia was meant to launch Russia's version of the space shuttle, *Buran*, into space. However, both the rocket and the space shuttle stopped production when the **Soviet Union** disbanded in 1991.

Sputnik II carried a dog named **Laika** onboard, making her the **first Earthling to be sent into space**.

The **Soyuz rocket** is the **ONLY** launch vehicle that transports people to the ISS.

A Proton rocket carrying a U.S. Intelsat-22 satellite made by Boeing Space Systems launched on March 25, 2012.

The United States Rocket Program

While Russia was developing its rockets, the United States also was inventing new rocket technology, including multi-stage rockets. In the past, rockets used a single engine to travel. When the rocket ran out of fuel, it stopped gaining speed. This limited the distance the rocket could travel. The United States decided to make rockets that had two stages, each with its own fuel. The bottom part of the rocket carried the greatest amount of fuel and pushed the rocket the farthest distance. When its fuel ran out, the bottom dropped away, and the top used its own fuel to keep moving forward.

Over time, more stages were used to make rockets that could reach farther distances. In 1958, a four-stage rocket was used to launch the first U.S. satellite, *Explorer I*, into space.

The United States government decided to create an organization that would develop technology for space exploration. In 1958, President Eisenhower announced the creation of NASA. This was followed by the construction of the Kennedy Space Center at Cape Canaveral, Florida.

President Eisenhower signed the National Aeronautics and Space Act into law on July 29, and NASA officially started operations on October 1.

THE SPACE RACE

With the launching of *Sputnik I*, Russia became the first country to send a satellite into space. The United States, however, was only a few months behind in sending *Explorer I* into space. Both countries had been working toward the same goal at the same time. When Russia had the first success story, the two countries began competing in what became known as the space race.

The space race lasted for 12 years, from 1957 to 1969. The ultimate goal of the race was to be the first country to put a human on the Moon. To accomplish this goal, both countries made many types of rockets that were meant to carry people and equipment into space. These included the Atlas and Titan rockets from the United States, and the R-7, Vostok, and Soyuz rockets from Russia.

The first Americans to walk on the Moon were part of the Apollo 11 mission.

Fly Me to the Moon

In 1961, President John F. Kennedy gave NASA a **mandate** to put two people on the Moon before 1970. This launched NASA's *Apollo* space program. The main goal of this program was to create a spacecraft that could carry three people into space, land on the Moon, and then bring the people back to Earth.

Before sending people to the Moon, NASA sent robots to find out as much as possible about the surface. Atlas missiles were used to send robot explorers to the surface of the Moon. The Atlas was the most powerful rocket of its time, producing a thrust of about 175 tons (159 t).

On Earth, scientists were constructing a plan to land people on the Moon. Part of this plan included the building of a powerful rocket. Wernher von Braun designed the Saturn V, a three-stage rocket, to do the job.

Each of the rocket stages was built at different places across the United States and were brought to the Kennedy Space Center for assembly. To stack together the stages of the Saturn V and prepare it for launch, NASA built a giant shed at the northern end of Cape Canaveral called the Vehicle Assembly Building, or VAB.

Covering 8 acres (3.2 hectares), the VAB was one of the largest buildings in the world when it was completed in 1965.

The stages of the Saturn V were put together on a mobile launch platform. Upon completion, the Saturn V was 363 feet (111 meters) tall—60 feet (18 m) taller than the Statue of Liberty on its pedestal. It weighed 3,000 tons (2,722 t) fully fueled.

The *Apollo* spacecraft was lifted by crane from the floor of the VAB and placed on top of Saturn V's third stage. A specially designed vehicle was driven under the mobile launch platform. The vehicle lifted the mobile platform, complete with Saturn V rocket, and slowly drove the Saturn V to the launch pad, 3 miles (4.8 km) away. When the vehicle arrived at the pad, it lowered Saturn V onto it. The crawler then backed out from under the mobile platform, and the rocket was ready for launch. At liftoff, Saturn V produced a thrust of more than 3,750 tons (3,402 t). This was enough to send the *Apollo* spacecraft to the Moon, where it landed on July 20, 1969. With this success, the United States became the winner of the space race.

Apollo 11 launched from Launch Complex 39 on July 16, 1969.

Delivery Trucks in Orbit

During the 1970s, NASA developed the space shuttle to replace all ELVs. The shuttle would launch satellites and spacecraft and return satellites to Earth for repair. Flights began in 1981, but the shuttle became too expensive to use for launching satellites, so its last mission took place in 2011. For this reason, ELVs continue to be used today. They act as delivery trucks, carrying satellites and spacecraft to different orbits.

Space shuttle *Atlantis* took only 8.5 minutes to reach speeds of 17,000 miles (27,359 km) per hour.

DRAGON

SpaceX also has a spacecraft called the Dragon. It was created to carry people and cargo to orbiting destinations. In 2012, it brought cargo to the ISS and safely returned cargo to Earth. This was the first time such an achievement had ever been made by a commercial spacecraft.

Plans are currently being made for Dragon to start carrying people. It will undertake its first manned test flight in 2018. In addition to flying astronauts to and from the ISS, Dragon may also start flying private space tourists around the Moon. This would help bridge the gap to SpaceX's ultimate goal of establishing a human colony on Mars.

In 2002, a company called SpaceX was founded. Its goal is to allow humans to live on other planets in the future. SpaceX is currently working on the world's most powerful operational rocket. Called Falcon Heavy, the rocket is capable of lifting more than two times as much as the next closest operational vehicle. Falcon Heavy is more affordable to run as well, operating at one-third the cost. It is scheduled for takeoff in mid-2017.

NASA is also working on a heavy lift rocket called the Space Launch System (SLS). It will be able to lift more weight than Falcon Heavy. However, launch costs for the SLS are much higher. The SLS is currently expected to launch in late 2018.

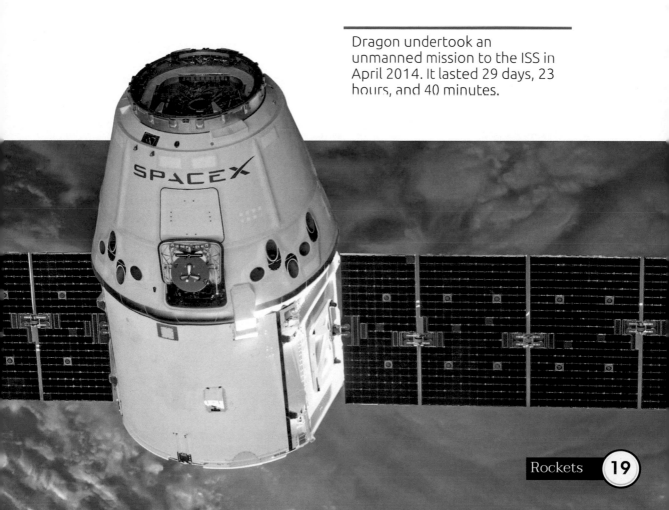

Dragon undertook an unmanned mission to the ISS in April 2014. It lasted 29 days, 23 hours, and 40 minutes.

Making the Grade

Working with rockets requires people to have very specific skills and education. Rocket specialists must have a good grasp of science principles, along with strong technical skills. They must be detail-oriented people who strive to improve current technologies. With these traits and qualifications, there are many career paths that can be taken.

QUALIFICATIONS TO BE A NASA ASTRONAUT

CITIZENSHIP
Pilots and mission specialists must be U.S. citizens. Payload specialists can be from other countries.

HEIGHT
Pilots must be 62 to 75 inches (157.5 to 190.5 centimeters) tall. Mission or payload specialists must be 58.5 to 76 inches (148.5 to 193 cm) tall.

HEALTH
All astronauts must pass a NASA physical, with specific vision and blood pressure requirements.

EDUCATION
Astronauts must have a minimum bachelor's degree in engineering, biology, physics, or mathematics. Most astronauts have a **doctorate**.

EXPERIENCE
Astronauts must have at least three years of experience in a science-related field. Pilots must have jet experience with more than 1,000 hours of in-command flight time.

ASTRONAUTICAL ENGINEER Astronautical engineers design, develop, and test spacecraft and rockets. They often specialize in very specific areas, such as structural design and navigation or communication systems. It is their job to create equipment and vehicles that can survive the journey from Earth to space and back again. They need to have expert knowledge on the conditions the equipment will experience so that the correct materials and technology are used to create it. They are involved in the construction process from design to finished product.

ROCKET TECHNICIAN Rocket technicians are involved in putting rockets together. Their work is very detailed and must be done properly so that the rocket meets all safety standards. They must inspect all of the parts that will be assembled to make sure that there are no flaws that could cause problems during launch. When the safety of the rocket is confirmed, the technicians are responsible for transporting it safely to the launch pad. They then assist in the final launch preparations so that the launch runs smoothly.

PILOT ASTRONAUT A pilot astronaut guides spacecraft into space and brings it back to Earth. These astronauts are responsible for the safety of the vehicle, the equipment inside, and the crew. Pilot astronauts must have strong knowledge about the scientific processes that propel their spacecraft into space and be able to apply this knowledge to the launch, flight, and landing of the spacecraft. Many pilot astronauts have engineering degrees for this reason.

A Day in Space

When astronauts go into space, they work as part of a NASA team. A day in space usually has a set schedule. The crew will awake to either the sound of an alarm clock, or the blast of a song over the speaker system. After eating breakfast, it is time for the astronauts to brush their teeth and get ready for work.

A list, known as the flight plan, tells the crew what they are to work on each day. Sometimes, there is need for a spacewalk. Other times, the crew carries out housekeeping duties, such as trash collection and cleaning. Breaks, such as lunch and dinner, are also scheduled throughout the day. Keeping fit in such a confined space is very important as well, so blocks of time are put aside for the astronauts to set up and use exercise equipment. At the end of the workday, the astronauts may read a book, listen to music, watch a movie, or check emails.

The crews of STS-131 and Expedition 23 came together at the ISS while space shuttle *Discovery* was docked there.

THE DAILY SCHEDULE

8:30 to 10:00 a.m.
Postsleep (Morning station inspection, breakfast, morning **hygiene**)

10:00 to 10:30 a.m.
Planning and coordination (Daily planning conference and status report)

 10:30 a.m. to 1:00 p.m.
Exercise (Set-up exercise equipment, exercise, and put equipment away)

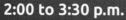

 1:00 to 2:00 p.m.
Lunch, personal hygiene

2:00 to 3:30 p.m.
Daily systems operations (Work preparation, report writing, emails, to-do list review, trash collection)

3:30 to 10:00 p.m.
Work (Work set-up and maintenance, performing experiments and payload operations, checking positioning and operating systems)

10:00 p.m. to 12:00 a.m.
Pre-sleep (food preparation, evening meal, and hygiene)

 12:00 to 8:30 a.m.
Sleep

Rocketing the World

Today, many countries and organizations around the world have space programs. The Ariane, a very powerful ELV, was one of the first projects from the **European Space Agency (ESA)**. Europeans began working on the Ariane series of ELVs in the early 1970s, when NASA first started making the shuttle. Ariane was designed to put communication satellites in space so that they could relay their television, telephone, and radio signals around the planet. First launched in 1979, the original Ariane I has been developed into the powerful Ariane 5 that is in use today. To date, Ariane has launched almost half of the world's commercial satellites.

Ariane 5 completed the last launch of 2016 for the ESA on December 21. It took off from Kourou, French Guiana, carrying two satellites called Star One and Sky Perfect.

China has already launched people into space, only the third country after Russia and the United States to do so. The first Chinese astronaut was launched into space on October 15, 2003. That was followed by a two-man flight two years later that lasted almost five days.

Some people see the greatest advantage of space programs as the co-operation they encourage between different people around the world. Rockets and satellite launchers have helped make that possible.

China's first female astronaut was a fighter pilot named Liu Yang. She went into space on the Shenzhou 9 spacecraft in June 2012.

Rocket History

The first rockets were made hundreds of years ago. Over time, they advanced from simple fireworks to complex rockets capable of space travel. This timeline highlights some of the major achievements in the history of the rocket.

1800s In later centuries, Europeans developed the rocket further as a weapon of war. One rocket was called the Congreve. It used a 16-foot (5-m) guide stick as a **stabilizer**. This helped the rocket travel distances up to 9,000 feet (2,743 m).

1926 American Robert Goddard was the first person to build a liquid-propellant rocket. It had long been known that liquid-propellant rockets would produce more energy than a solid propellant rocket, but no one had been able to build one. Goddard studied the problems associated with getting a liquid rocket to fly and successfully launched the first liquid-fueled rocket.

1200 to 1300 AD The first rockets were used in China about 800 years ago. Fueled by gunpowder, they were first used as fireworks at parties and gatherings. Later, the Chinese adapted them for use in warfare.

FIRST NASA DIRECTOR

Wernher von Braun was born in Wirzitz, Germany, on March 12, 1912. After reading science fiction books by Jules Verne and H.G. Wells, he developed an interest in space travel. In school, he worked on mastering mathematics so that he could learn the science behind rocketry. When he finished high school, von Braun was accepted into the Berlin Institute of Technology to study engineering. Upon graduation in 1932, von Braun went to work for the German army. His job was to create rockets for the military. While working on these projects, he continued his studies and, in 1934, received a doctorate in aerospace engineering from the University of Berlin.

Wernher von Braun continued his work with the German army in the years leading up to World War II. In 1937, he was sent to a secret site on the Baltic Coast to develop missiles for the war. It was here that the V-2 missile was developed.

1942 During World War II, German engineer Wernher von Braun created a rocket missile called the V-2. It traveled so fast and far that it became a main weapon for the Germans throughout the war.

1945 Following the war, von Braun moved to the United States to make rockets for them. There, he developed the Redstone, the first missile built in America to achieve a range of more than 200 miles (322 km).

1960 Von Braun joined NASA, where he worked on making rockets for space travel.

A Redstone Rocket has been on display in the town square of Warren, New Hampshire, since the early 1970s.

Following his move to the United States, von Braun continued designing military rockets. However, when NASA was created, he became the agency's first director, and his focus turned to developing rockets that would go into space. von Braun had many successes with NASA and played a key role in their rocket program until his retirement in 1972. In 1977, he died of cancer at the age of 65.

Rockets Quiz

1

How many main systems does a rocket have?

2

Why was the Dragon spacecraft created?

3

On what date was the first space shuttle launched?

4

How tall was Saturn V upon completion?

5

Which launch vehicle transports people to the ISS?

6
What does NASA stand for?

7
Where were the first rockets used?

9
Which country launched the first successful satellite?

8
How long did the space race last?

10
Who was China's first female astronaut?

Key Words

atmosphere: the layer of gases that surrounds Earth

ballistic missile: a type of rocket that has no wings and stays on course when its power source is used up

cylindrical: shaped like a tube

doctorate: an advanced university degree

European Space Agency (ESA): an organization formed to develop Europe's space capabilities

expendable: able to be used up and discarded

hygiene: the process of keeping clean

mandate: an official command

missiles: rocket-propelled weapons mobile launch

oxidizer: something that undergoes a chemical reaction with oxygen

platform: a structure that is used to move the space shuttle from the assembly building to the launch pad

propellants: fuels for a liquid rocket

resin: a waxlike substance

satellites: spacecraft that move in orbit around Earth, the Moon, or other bodies in space and send signals to Earth

Soviet Union: a former communist country in eastern Europe and northern Asia that was established in 1922 and officially dissolved in 1991

stabilizer: a device that keeps an object balanced and steady

thrust: the force that occurs when an object is pushed

Index

Log on to www.av2books.com

AV² by Weigl brings you media enhanced books that support active learning. Go to www.av2books.com, and enter the special code found on page 2 of this book. You will gain access to enriched and enhanced content that supplements and complements this book. Content includes video, audio, weblinks, quizzes, a slide show, and activities.

AV² Online Navigation

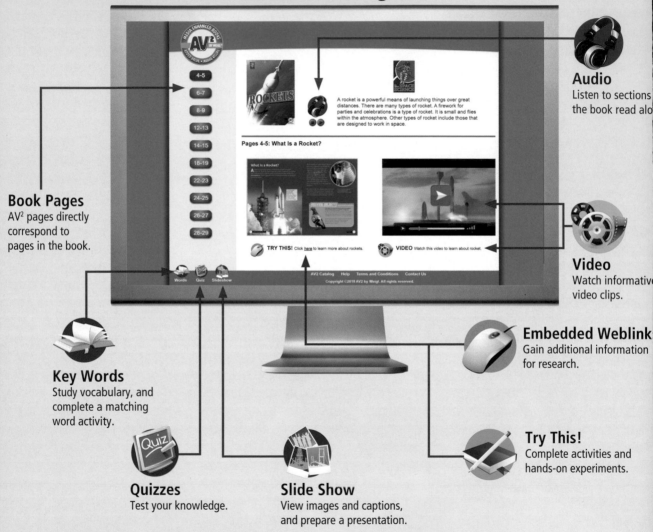

Book Pages
AV² pages directly correspond to pages in the book.

Audio
Listen to sections the book read alo

Video
Watch informative video clips.

Embedded Weblink
Gain additional information for research.

Try This!
Complete activities and hands-on experiments.

Key Words
Study vocabulary, and complete a matching word activity.

Quizzes
Test your knowledge.

Slide Show
View images and captions, and prepare a presentation.

AV² was built to bridge the gap between print and digital. We encourage you to tell us what you like and what you want to see in the future.

Sign up to be an AV² Ambassador at www.av2books.com/ambassador.

Due to the dynamic nature of the Internet, some of the URLs and activities provided as part of AV² by Weigl may have changed or ceased to exist. AV² by Weigl accepts no responsibility for any such changes. All media enhanced books are regularly monitored to update addresses and sites in a timely manner. Contact AV² by Weigl at 1-866-649-3445 or av2books@weigl.com with any questions, comments, or feedback.